CEN-MED

Date Due

APR 28 '99			
OCT 13 '99			
MAR 3 0			
MAY 4			
JUL 5			
NOV 0 2 '00			
PR 30 '02			

SCIENCE PROJECT IDEAS

Science Project Ideas About
TREES

Robert Gardner

Enslow Publishers, Inc.

44 Fadem Road	PO Box 38
Box 699	Aldershot
Springfield, NJ 07081	Hants GU12 6BP
USA	UK

Library of Congress Cataloging-in-Publication Data

Gardner, Robert, 1929–
    Science project ideas about trees / Robert Gardner.
        p. cm.—(Science project ideas)
    Includes bibliographical references and index.
    Summary: Contains many experiments introducing the processes that
take place in plants and trees.
    ISBN 0-89490-846-4
    1. Trees—Juvenile literature. 2. Trees—Experiments—Juvenile
literature. 3. Botany projects—Juvenile literature. [1. Trees. 2. Trees—
Experiments. 3. Experiments. 4. Science projects.] I. Title. II. Series:
Gardner, Robert, 1929– Science project ideas.
QK475.8.G36 1997
582.16' 078—dc2l   97-6515
                                                   CIP
                                                   AC

Printed in the United States of America

10 9 8 7 6 5 4 3 2 1

Illustration Credits: Jacob Katari

Photo Credits: David Webster, pp. 20, 77, 79; Robert Gardner, p. 31.

Cover Photo: Jerry McCrea

CONTENTS

INTRODUCTION

In this book you will find experiments and information about trees, one of the world's most important types of plants. The experiments use simple everyday materials you can find at home or at school.

The book will help you to work the way real scientists do. You will be answering questions by doing experiments to understand basic scientific principles or techniques.

Most of the experiments will provide detailed guidance. But some of them will raise questions and ask you to make up your own experiments to answer them. This is the kind of experiment that could be a particularly good start for a science fair project. Such experiments are marked with an asterisk (*).

Please note: **If an experiment uses anything that has a potential for danger, you will be asked to work with an adult.** *Please do so! The purpose of this teamwork is to prevent you from being hurt.*

Science Project Ideas About Trees can open science's door for you while you enjoy the shade of a large tree or periodically measure the growth of a tree you have planted.

MEASUREMENT ABBREVIATIONS

centimeter	cm	inch	in
cubic centimeter	cu cm	kilogram	kg
cubic foot	cu ft	liter	l
cubic meter	cu m	meter	m
degrees Celsius	°C	milliliter	ml
degrees Fahrenheit	°F	ounce	oz
foot	ft	pound	lb
gallon	gal	square centimeter	sq cm
gram	g		

The maple puts on her corals in May.
(James Russell Lowell)

1

Trees: A Vital Part of Our World

Can you imagine a world without trees? If you live on a prairie or in the desert, you probably can. But then stop and think. Can you imagine a world without paper, certain fruits and nuts, or lumber and wooden furniture? For without trees there would be no newspapers and books, no apples and oranges, no walnuts and chestnuts, and no wood for buildings and furniture. People who depend on wood for fuel would be without heat and unable to cook their food. It would be a very different world.

Trees are defined as plants that have a single sturdy, woody, permanent stem and grow taller than most other plants. Such a definition is used to distinguish trees from shrubs and bushes, which have many stems and don't grow very tall. But you know what trees are, and you can probably identify many of the trees that grow in the region where you live.

Biologists divide trees into two groups— gymnosperms and angiosperms. Trees that are gymnosperms are commonly called evergreens, conifers, or softwoods. They include pines, spruces, firs, hemlocks, and other trees with needlelike leaves. The word *gymnosperm* means "naked seed." Gymnosperms produce seeds on scales. The scales are often grouped together as cones. When the seeds of gymnosperms mature and fall, they are not covered, but are exposed to the air.

Trees that are angiosperms, on the other hand, produce flowers. The seeds, which form within the flowers, are covered by a part of the flower's pistil known as the ovary. (Figure 1 shows a typical flower.) As the ovary ripens, it becomes the fruit of the tree. An apple, for example, contains the ripened ovary of an apple blossom. Inside the apple are the seeds.

FIGURE 1

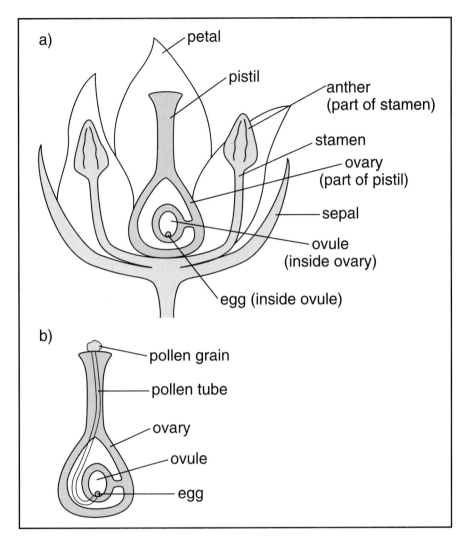

a) A cross section of a typical flower shows the pistil and stamens. The ovary of the pistil contains one or more ovules. Within an ovule is the egg. The anthers of the stamens produce the pollen.

b) When pollen is deposited on a pistil, a tube grows from the pollen, through the pistil, to the egg inside the ovule of the ovary. Sperm move through the pollen tube to unite with the egg.

On the outside of the apple you can find traces of its origin from a flower. Look in the dent on the bottom of an apple. There you can see five tiny dry points—the remains of the leaves (sepals) that once held a flower.

Trees that are angiosperms are often referred to as deciduous trees because they lose their leaves for part of the year. (*Deciduous* comes from a Latin word meaning "to fall.") They are also called hardwoods because they produce wood that is harder than the wood of gymnosperms.

The flowers of angiosperms have stamens that produce pollen. The pollen is transferred, often by wind or insects, to the pistil of another flower. There the pollen generates a pollen tube with sperm cells that reach the egg cell or egg cells in the flower's ovary. The fertilized egg becomes the seed, which is surrounded by the ripened ovary—the fruit of the plant. Sometimes the fruit is large and edible, as is true of apples, oranges, peaches, and pears. Other times it is simply a thin cover, like the winged cases that enclose the seeds of maple trees, or a pod, like the pods that cover peas.

Many trees have small flowers that go unnoticed. The best time to look for them is in the spring just as the landscape begins to turn green. A red maple's tiny red flowers appear just before the leaves come out. The fruit consists of a pair of "wings." When the seeds fall, the wings make the seeds spin and a wind may cause them to land some distance from the tree on which they grew.

Oak flowers are small, but the fruit of oak trees is the familiar acorn so loved by squirrels. The flowers of birch trees are long thin catkins. (They are called catkins because they resemble a cat's tail.) Each birch tree produces two distinct types of flowers: male or staminate flowers with only stamens, and female or pistillate flowers with only pistils. Many other kinds of trees also produce separate male and female flowers. In some species, a single tree produces only staminate flowers or only pistillate flowers.

Tree Parts

 Trees have four distinct parts: (1) the stem, or trunk, with its branches and twigs; (2) the leaves where the trees manufacture food; (3) the roots, which support the rest of the tree and grow down into the soil where they absorb water and minerals; and (4) the flowers of angiosperms and cones of gymnosperms, which enable trees to reproduce.

The Stem

The stem or trunk of a tree provides both support and a system of tubes. The tubes transport water and minerals upward and provide a downward path for foods.

The outer part of the stem is the bark. The bark is made up of two parts (see Figure 2). The outer bark contains dead cells that protect the living tissues within it. The inner bark contains living cells. Together, these inner cells are known as the phloem. The phloem lies next to a thin layer of cells called the cambium. The layer of cells that make up the cambium produces phloem cells on its outer side and another type of cell, called xylem, on its inner side. The xylem contains a number of different kinds of cells. Some xylem cells are used to transport water and minerals and some food upward from the roots to the leaves. Other xylem cells move water, food, and minerals horizontally across the stem. These are called ray cells. Many xylem cells have thick walls that help to support the growing tree.

Phloem carries mostly food manufactured in the leaves down to the cells of the stem and roots. The role of phloem in conducting food was determined by experiment. When a ring of bark and phloem was removed from a tree trunk, water still reached the leaves above the cut, but food did not reach the cells of the roots or stem below the cut. As a result, the roots eventually died and could no longer absorb water and minerals from the soil. The tree died. The experiment showed that water must move upward to the stem and leaves through the xylem, while food moves downward from the leaves through the phloem.

FIGURE 2

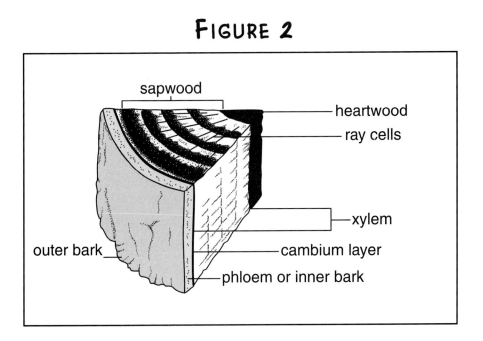

The drawing shows a section of a tree trunk. Heartwood and sapwood are inside the cambium layer. Phloem cells lie outside the cambium. The outer bark is made up of dead cells that are constantly being shed.

In older trees, the inner xylem is called the heartwood. Heartwood is made up of dead cells that are filled with substances that provide a strong inner core. The cells of the heartwood no longer carry materials up the tree. The outer part of the xylem is the sapwood. It lies between the cambium layer and the heartwood. It is the xylem cells in the sapwood that move water and minerals upward through a tree to the leaves.

The Leaves

Leaves are the part of the tree where food is produced by a process known as photosynthesis. Leaves are green because they contain chlorophyll. Chlorophyll makes leaves green because it reflects green light and absorbs the other colors in sunlight. Chlorophyll enables plants to combine carbon dioxide and water to form sugar. Carbon dioxide is found in air and enters the underside of leaves through tiny openings called stomates (see Figure 3). Water is absorbed from soil through the roots and passes upward through xylem cells to the leaves. In the presence of chlorophyll and light, the carbon dioxide and water in a leaf are combined to form sugar. Much of the sugar

FIGURE 3

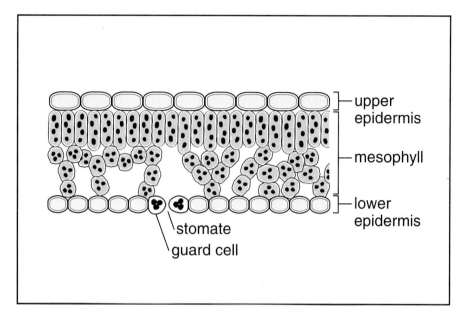

A microscopic view of the edge of a leaf is shown. The actual thickness is less than a millimeter. The upper and lower epidermis are cells that protect the inner mesophyll cells where photosynthesis takes place. The stomate is one of many such openings through the underside of the leaf. Each stomate is surrounded by guard cells. When the guard cells lose water during dry weather, they close the stomate.

is converted to starch and then stored in plant cells until it is needed.

During the process of photosynthesis, the energy in sunlight is changed to the chemical energy stored in the food produced. The by-product of this process is oxygen, the gas that humans and animals need to release the energy stored in the food they eat.

It is through the stomates that water evaporates from leaves and enters the atmosphere. This process, called transpiration, accounts for a vast amount of water that passes from the ground through plants and into the air. To produce 1 kg of dry corn, a plant must absorb 350 kg (770 lbs) of water. One kilogram of wheat requires 500 kg (1,100 lbs) of water, and 900 kg (2,000 lbs) of water are needed to form 1 kg (2.2 lbs) of dry alfalfa. Most of the water absorbed by these plants evaporates into the atmosphere.

During droughts, the water content of the guard cells that surround the stomates decreases. This causes the shape of the cells to change, closing or narrowing the stomatal openings. With the stomates closed, transpiration decreases and less water is lost to the atmosphere.

Roots

A tree's roots absorb water and minerals from the soil and transport them to the stem and leaves. But roots also have another function. The larger roots hold the tree firmly in the soil. If you have ever seen a tree blowing in a strong wind, you realize how important it is for the tree to be firmly anchored to the ground.

Flowers and Cones

Trees that are angiosperms produce flowers. Flowers are the reproductive parts of a plant (see Figure 1). The stamens, or male parts of the flower, produce the pollen that gives rise to sperm cells. The pistils produce the ovules that contain the egg cells. Some trees have flowers that contain both stamens and pistils. Other types of trees have separate flowers for stamens (staminate flowers) and pistils (pistillate flowers). In some species, the same tree will have staminate flowers on one branch and pistillate flowers on another branch. In other species, the trees will produce either pistillate or staminate flowers, but not both.

The cones of gymnosperms produce either pollen or ovules. However, both male and female cones are located on the same tree. In the spring of the year, vast amounts of pollen are produced by pine trees. The fine yellow dust you find on walks or at the edge of evaporating mud puddles in the spring is probably pine pollen.

Tree Growth, Distribution, and Life Cycle

 Trees grow in diameter. We can see this by looking at the annual rings on a tree stump. Each year the cambium layer of cells in the stem produces new phloem cells on its outer side and new xylem cells on its inner side. The xylem cells produced in the spring are large and thin-walled. They make up the lighter part of an annual ring. The xylem cells produced in the summer are smaller with thick walls. Summerwood is the dark part of each annual ring.

At the tips of roots and branches are tissues that also produce new cells. It is these cells that cause the tree to grow downward, outward, and upward. But trees get longer only at these growing tips. A point on the trunk of a tree where a branch has formed will not move upward. It will remain at the same height above the ground.

The growth of a tree begins with a seed. The germinating seed is called a seedling. If it survives, it will produce its own pollen and/or ovules after ten or more years. It can then produce its own seeds and complete the life cycle as it gives rise to a new generation of its species.

Theoretically, trees are immortal, but the oldest known trees are less than 5,000 years old. Most trees do not live more than a century. Forest fires destroy many trees. Others are blown down by high winds, are struck by lightning, die during a drought, or are cut down by humans or beavers. Trees are also subject to fungal diseases such as Dutch elm disease, chestnut blight, white-pine blister rust, and many more. Sometimes trees are lost to insects that cause them to rot.

Trees first evolved on this planet in a tropical climate where the seasons were not marked by large temperature changes. As the earth's climate changed, the trees in temperate zones, such as North America, adapted to the seasons. They developed some kind of internal "clock" that told them when it was safe to put out new leaves, shoots, and flowers in the spring. The same clock told them when it was time to shed their leaves and become dormant for the cold winter to come.

Evergreens, such as fir and pine trees, are generally able to withstand the cold better than deciduous trees, which shed their leaves in the fall. That is why you will find evergreens in northern Canada and Alaska (see Figure 4) and at high altitudes where temperatures are low. But even evergreens have their limits. They will not grow in regions where temperatures fall to -45°C (-49°F) in the winter.

FIGURE 4

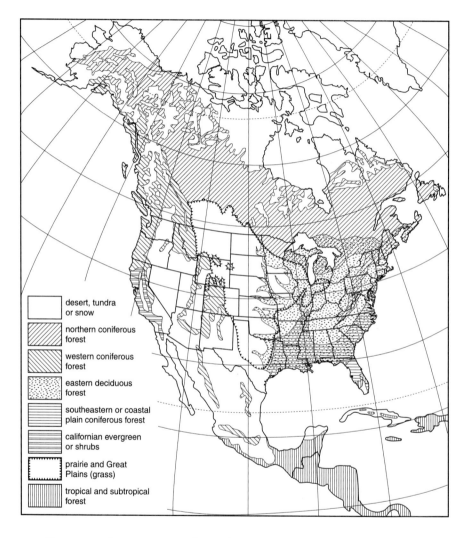

desert, tundra or snow

northern coniferous forest

western coniferous forest

eastern deciduous forest

southeastern or coastal plain coniferous forest

californian evergreen or shrubs

prairie and Great Plains (grass)

tropical and subtropical forest

The major forest areas of North and Central America are shown on this map. Some of the areas overlap. For example, both conifers (evergreens) and deciduous trees (trees that lose their leaves) are found around the Great Lakes.

In addition to favorable temperatures, trees must have moisture and proper soil conditions. Gentle winds help to spread pollen and replenish the carbon dioxide used in photosynthesis. But high winds may remove moisture from trees and reduce growth. Of course, the range of conditions that different trees can tolerate varies. Figure 4 shows the major types of forest areas of North and Central America. In Africa, South and Central America, and southeast Asia, there are extensive rain forests. Some of these rain forests are being destroyed by logging or by burning to make way for more agriculture.

How Trees Are Used

 Trees play very important roles in our lives. In addition to the shade and beauty they offer, trees hold soil in place and reduce erosion caused by floods or heavy rains. Through photosynthesis, trees provide the food they need to maintain their own growth. In many cases, they also produce the food that makes up the fruits and nuts that are a vital part of our diets. Trees are essential to the paper industry where they are used for the wood pulp from which paper is made. In many parts of the world, wood is the

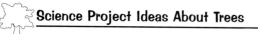
FIGURE 5

As this photograph shows, wood has one major flaw as a building material.

primary fuel for heating and cooking. And it is from trees that we obtain the lumber used to build homes and other buildings. As the photograph in Figure 5 shows, wood has one major drawback as a building material. Despite its flammability, a lot of wood is sawed into lumber because it is light and easy to cut, shape, smooth, and join together. Trees or their wood are also the source of many substances such as rubber, cellulose, tannins, and resins, which are refined into products such as turpentine.

You cannot see the wood for the trees.
(John Heywood)

2

TREES OF ALL KINDS

Foresters often measure trees to find out how much lumber can be obtained from the tree. To do this they need to know the tree's height and diameter. A tree's height is also an indicator of its age. If you know the average amount that a particular species of tree grows each year, its height will give you a rough idea of its age. The same is true of a tree's diameter.

The cells of the older wood near the center of a tree are dead. They form the

FIGURE 6

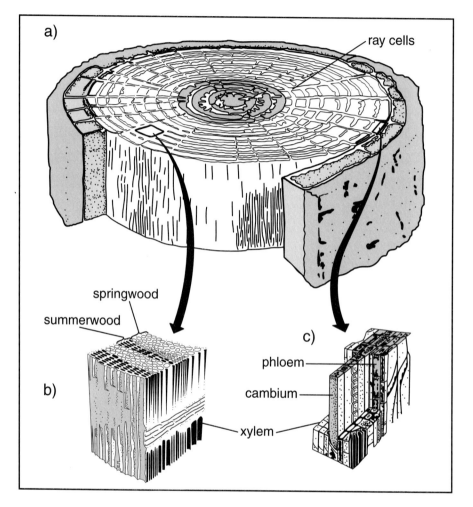

a) The drawing shows a section of a tree trunk. The dark wood at the center consists of dead cells filled with dark-colored substances. This is the heartwood. The ray cells, which together look like the spokes of a wheel, carry food and water across the trunk.

b) This drawing shows an enlarged segment of two annual rings.

c) The cambium produces xylem cells on its inside and phloem cells on its outside. It accounts for the sideways growth of the stem.

tree's heartwood. If air can reach the heartwood, it decays and the tree becomes hollow. Hollow trees can live for many years, but they lack the heartwood's strength.

The sapwood surrounding the heartwood is made up of xylem cells that carry water and minerals up the tree. Most sap flows in the new (most recently formed) ring of xylem cells. If these cells become blocked by a fungus, as they do in Dutch elm disease, the tree may die. The older sapwood cannot carry enough fluid to keep the tree alive. Figure 6 shows a tree's heartwood and sapwood.

The wood of each species of tree has its characteristic color, odor, taste, texture, and grain. Descriptive terms such as "ebony black" and "ash-blonde" reveal the color of the wood of these two trees. And carpenters know that oakwood is yellow, locust is bronze, and the wood of the red fir is actually white.

Experiment *2.1

HOW BIG IS THAT TREE?

To do this experiment you will need:

- ✔ rope
- ✔ meterstick (yardstick)
- ✔ tall trees
- ✔ sun
- ✔ a friend
- ✔ pencil

There are several ways to measure a tree. One way is to measure its height. Another way is to measure the thickness (diameter) of its trunk. Still another way is to measure its girth—the distance around the tree's trunk, or its circumference. Some trees grow very tall. Some redwood trees grow to heights of more than 100 m (330 ft). The circumferences of sequoia (Sierran redwood) trees may reach nearly 30 m (98 ft), which means their trunks are 9 m (30 ft) in diameter.

Look for the biggest tree around your school or neighborhood. You can measure the tree's circumference with a piece of rope and a meterstick, or yardstick (see Figure 7). Place the rope around the base of the tree's trunk.

FIGURE 7

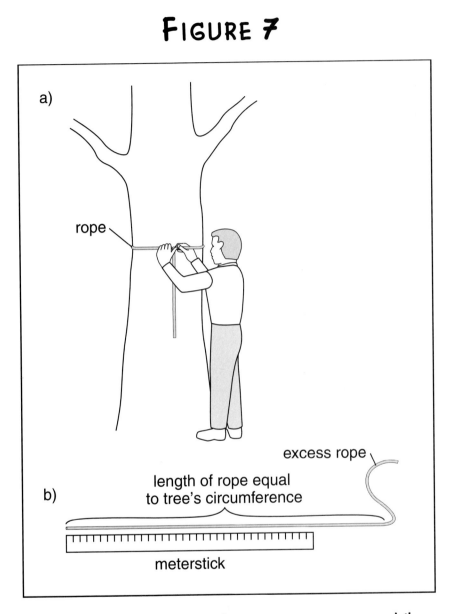

a) To measure a tree's circumference, wrap a rope around the tree at eye level. Mark the point where one end of the rope meets the rest of the rope.

b) Use a meterstick to measure the length of rope that matches the tree's circumference.

Pick up the ends of the rope and wiggle it back and forth until it is at eye level. Grip the rope at the point where one end meets the rest of the rope. Place the rope on the ground. Use the meterstick (yardstick) to measure the length of the rope that went around the tree. What was the circumference of the tree you measured?

Since most tree trunks are basically round (circular), it is not necessary to measure the diameter of a tree's trunk. You can calculate it from the tree's circumference. For any circle, the diameter is equal to the circumference divided by a constant number called π (pi). The value of π is approximately 3.14, but 3 is close enough for estimating the diameter of a tree, which is seldom a perfect circle. What is the approximate diameter of the tree you just measured?

There are several ways to find the height of a tree. If the sun is shining, you can use the length of the tree's shadow and the length of the shadow of an upright meterstick or yardstick to find the tree's height. The sun's light rays are nearly parallel when they reach the earth. As a result, the tree's height divided by the length of its shadow has the same value as the stick's height (100 cm) divided by the length of its shadow (see Figure 8a). Why must

FIGURE 8

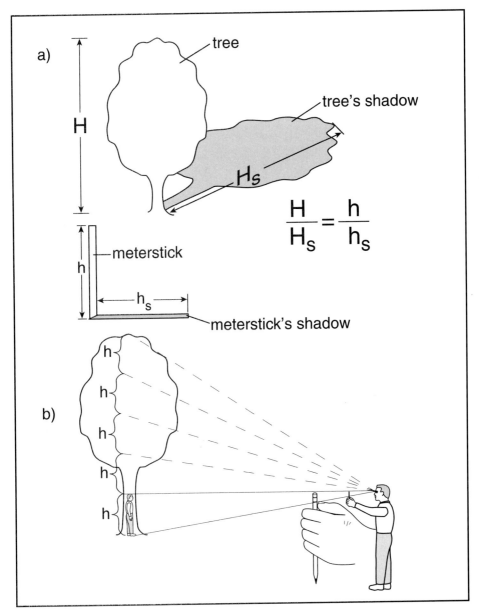

a) The shadow method can be used to calculate a tree's height.

b) The artist's method of estimating the height of a tree is shown. In the drawing, the tree is five times as tall as the person standing next to it.

both shadows be measured at approximately the same time?

Suppose the length of the meterstick's shadow is 50 cm. Then the height of the stick is twice the length of its shadow. The height of the tree, therefore, must also be twice the length of its shadow. If the tree's shadow is 10 m long, its height is 20 m. What will be the length of this tree's shadow when the meterstick casts a shadow that is 25 cm long?

If the sun is not shining, you can use a method used by artists to measure a tree's height. Have a friend stand next to the tree you want to measure, while you stand about 20 m (60–70 ft) away. Hold a pencil upright at arm's length, as shown in Figure 8b. Line up the top of the pencil with the top of your friend's head. Holding the pencil steady, move your thumb along the pencil until it is in line with the bottom of your friend's feet. The distance between your thumb and the top of the pencil represents your friend's height as seen from about 20 m away. Next, determine how many of these lengths are in the tree's height. You can do this by moving the pencil upward one length at a time.

By knowing how tall your friend is, you can find the approximate height of the tree. For example, suppose your friend is 1.5 m

(4 ft, 11 in) tall and the tree, according to your measurement with the pencil, is ten times as tall as your friend. The height of the tree must be:

10 x 1.5 m = 15 m, or 49 ft

Measure the height and circumference of a number of trees in the area where you live. Try to measure the heights of a number of different kinds (species) of trees such as maples, pines, oaks, poplars, or whatever species you can find. Choose trees with approximately the same diameter. Does one kind of tree seem to grow taller than others? Do any tend to be shorter than others? Design some experiments to find out if the location of a tree affects its height. For example, does a tree alone in an open area grow taller than trees of the same species growing in a cluster or in a forest? Design an experiment to find out whether or not trees of different species grow faster near water (ponds, lakes, or streams) than in drier soil.

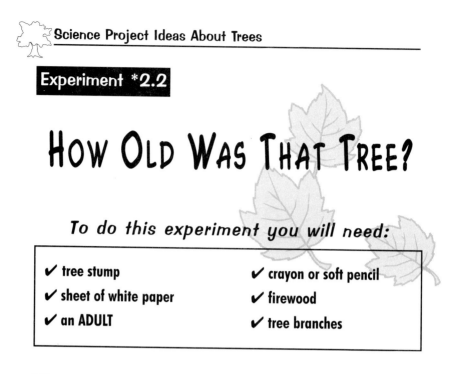

Experiment *2.2

HOW OLD WAS THAT TREE?

To do this experiment you will need:

✔ tree stump

✔ sheet of white paper

✔ an ADULT

✔ crayon or soft pencil

✔ firewood

✔ tree branches

The approximate age of a tree can be found by counting the annual rings, like those shown in the photograph in Figure 9. The tree adds a new ring every year. Each ring has two parts, as was shown in Figure 6b. The wider, lighter part (springwood) is made up of cells that are added in the spring when the tree grows rapidly. The thinner, darker part of the ring (summerwood) is formed during the rest of the year when the tree grows more slowly.

Unfortunately, you can't see the rings until the tree is cut down. Foresters and research scientists use fine augers (hollow drills) to cut out small cores from a tree. The cores can then be used to count the annual rings. But even the annual rings may not give a tree's exact

FIGURE 9

An old telephone pole, made from a tree, was cut into short segments to serve as posts. This photograph shows one end of a post. You can see the annual rings on the top of this post.

age. If a hurricane, tornado, or other event tears the leaves off a tree, the tree will sometimes grow and lose a second set of leaves in the same year. Such a tree will form two growth rings in the same year.

Even though you don't have the fine auger used to take core samples from a tree, you can still see annual rings. Find a tree stump. You will be able to see the annual rings and count them. How old was the tree before it was cut down? How can you tell the years during which the tree grew a lot? How can you tell the years during which the tree grew very little? How can trees be used to determine past weather patterns?

FIGURE 10

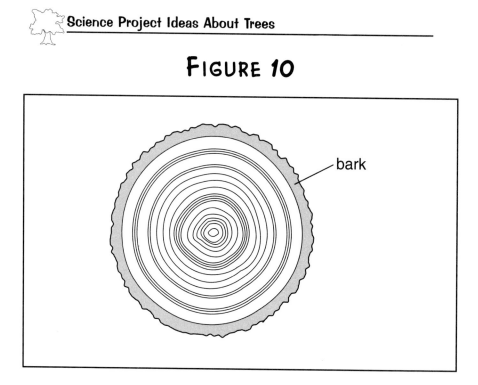

bark

How old was this tree when it was cut down? During which years did it grow a lot? During which years did it grow very little? Why do you think it grew more in some years than in others?

Use a sheet of white paper and a crayon or soft pencil to make a stump rubbing. Place the sheet of paper on the stump and hold it steady. Be sure the paper is large enough to cover the top of the stump. Rub the side of the crayon or the side of the pencil point back and forth over the paper across the entire stump. Can you see the annual rings in the rubbing?

You can also see annual rings on firewood. Look for these tree rings at the ends of unsplit logs in a woodpile. Can you tell the age of the tree from which the log came?

An adult may be willing to cut down a small tree so that you can look at the annual rings in the stump. **ASK THE ADULT** to cut some branches off the same tree. Do branches have annual rings? If they do, can you predict how the number of annual rings in higher branches will compare with the number in lower branches?

Look at the drawing of the top of a stump in Figure 10. How old was the tree when it was cut down? In which years did the tree grow rapidly? In which years did the tree grow slowly? What might have caused its slow growth?

Experiment *2.3

GROW YOUR OWN CHRISTMAS TREE

To do this experiment you will need:

- ✔ small tree such as a Norway spruce
- ✔ shovel
- ✔ soil
- ✔ tape measure
- ✔ meterstick (yardstick)
- ✔ graph paper

If you have a space near your home where you can plant a tree, you might like to buy a small spruce tree and plant it. The nursery where you buy the tree will tell you how to plant and nurture it. Each month you can measure your tree's height and the circumference of its trunk several inches above the ground. This information can be used to make a graph of the tree's growth. During what part of the year does the tree grow the most? Does it grow more some years than others? Can you explain why?

When it reaches a height of 8 ft or more, you might like to cut it, bring it inside, and decorate it for the holiday season. If you prefer not to cut it, you could dig it up during the autumn and transplant it into a large container that could be moved inside. (Talk to someone at a nursery to find out how to dig up a small tree for transplanting.) In the spring, you can replant it outside.

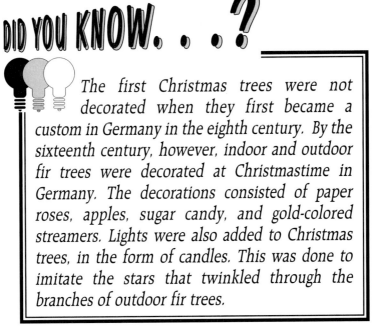

DID YOU KNOW. . .?

The first Christmas trees were not decorated when they first became a custom in Germany in the eighth century. By the sixteenth century, however, indoor and outdoor fir trees were decorated at Christmastime in Germany. The decorations consisted of paper roses, apples, sugar candy, and gold-colored streamers. Lights were also added to Christmas trees, in the form of candles. This was done to imitate the stars that twinkled through the branches of outdoor fir trees.

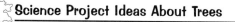

Experiment 2.4

TESTING WOOD FOR HARDNESS

To do this experiment you will need:

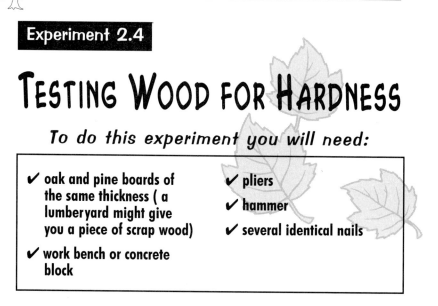

- ✔ oak and pine boards of the same thickness (a lumberyard might give you a piece of scrap wood)
- ✔ work bench or concrete block
- ✔ pliers
- ✔ hammer
- ✔ several identical nails

One way to test wood for hardness is to try to drive a nail into it. As you might expect, it is a lot easier to drive a nail into softwood than into hardwood.

Place pieces of oak and pine boards of the same thickness on a workbench or concrete block. To avoid any danger of hitting your hand, hold the nail with pliers. Use a hammer to drive identical nails into each kind of wood. Which wood seems to be harder? How can you tell? If possible, repeat the experiment with other types of wood. Which are hardwoods? Which are softwoods?

Wooden baseball bats, which are used in the major leagues, are made of ash. Do you think ash is a hardwood or a softwood? Why do you think so?

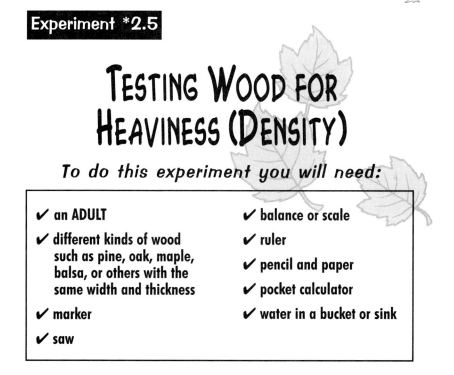

TESTING WOOD FOR HEAVINESS (DENSITY)

To do this experiment you will need:

- ✔ an ADULT
- ✔ different kinds of wood such as pine, oak, maple, balsa, or others with the same width and thickness
- ✔ marker
- ✔ saw
- ✔ balance or scale
- ✔ ruler
- ✔ pencil and paper
- ✔ pocket calculator
- ✔ water in a bucket or sink

Obtain samples of different kinds of wood such as pine, oak, maple, balsa, and/or others. If possible, obtain samples that have the same width and thickness. Label each sample with the name of the wood. Then **ASK AN ADULT** to saw the boards so that they are all the same length (about 4 in or smaller so they will fit on the pan of a balance or scale). If all the pieces of wood have the same dimensions (length, width, and height), their volumes are also the same. If their dimensions are not the same, you should skip the next two paragraphs and find the actual density.

Weigh the equal volumes of different kinds of wood on a balance or scale. Record the weight of each piece of wood. For the same volume, which wood is the heaviest? Which wood is the lightest? Does the wood's heaviness depend on whether it is a hardwood or a softwood?

When you compare the weights of the same volume of two or more things, you are comparing what is called their densities. Density is a measure of how compact a substance is. It tells you how much weight is packed into a certain volume. For objects with equal volumes, greater weight means greater density. From your weighings of equal volumes, you now know what the order of densities is for the different types of wood, from the most dense to the least dense.

To find the actual density, you can divide the weight of the wood by its volume. For example, if the piece of wood is 9.00 cm wide, 4.50 cm thick, and 10.00 cm long, its volume is:

> 9.00 cm x 4.50 cm x 10.00 cm =
> 405 cubic centimeters (cu cm)

If that piece of wood weighs 202 g, its density is:

> 202 g ÷ 405 cu cm =
> 0.499 g/cu cm

If all the pieces of wood you weighed had the same volume, you only have to measure the dimensions of one piece with a ruler to find the volume of all of them. If they did not have the same dimensions, you must calculate the volume of each kind of wood separately. Then, to find the wood's density, divide its weight by its volume. This will give you the density of each kind of wood in grams per cubic centimeter (g/cu cm), or ounces per cubic inch (oz/cu in).

The density of water is 1.0 g/cu cm. Which of these different kinds of wood do you think will float in water? Test your predictions by placing the different kinds of wood in water. Were your predictions correct?

Find an odd-shaped object that is made of wood. Design an experiment that would allow you to determine the density of the wooden object. Can you then use that information to identify the wood from which the object was made?

Table 1 shows the density of several different kinds of wood and the heat that can be obtained from each species when it is used for fuel. The density of the wood is measured in kg per cord. A cord is a stack of wood 8 ft (2.44 m) long, 4 ft (1.22 m) wide, and 4 ft (1.22 m) high; its volume is 128 cu ft (3.6 cu m). The

TABLE 1

DENSITY AND HEAT CONTENT OF DIFFERENT
KINDS OF WOOD

KIND OF WOOD	DENSITY OF WOOD (in kg per cord)	HEAT RELEASED PER CORD (in millions of Calories)
Hickory	2,000	7.9
Sugar maple	1,900	7.3
American beech	1,800	7.2
White ash	1,700	6.6
Paper birch	1,500	5.9
Douglas fir	1,300	5.4
Eastern white pine	1,000	4.0

heat released by burning a cord of wood is measured in Calories. A Calorie, or kilocalorie, is the amount of heat needed to raise the temperature of 1.0 kg of water by 1ºC.

How does the density of hickory compare with the density of eastern white pine? How does the heat produced by burning a cord of hickory compare with the heat produced by burning a cord of eastern white pine? In general, as the density of wood decreases, what happens to the quantity of heat that can be obtained by burning a cord of the wood? Would you expect to obtain more heat from a cord of hardwood or a cord of softwood? Is the density of a single piece of wood smaller or larger than the values of stacked wood given here? What makes you think so?

When all the world is young, lad,
And all the trees are green . . .
(Charles Kingsley)

3

LEAVES: A TREE'S FOOD FACTORY

A tree's food production takes place in its leaves. While the tree's stem and roots are permanent structures, the leaves are temporary. Most leaves do not survive for more than six months. It is through the leaves, too, that trees lose water. Evaporation of water from leaves enables trees to lift water to heights of 100 m (330 ft). The forces that hold molecules of water together (surface tension) are so great that water at the top of a tree pulls on the molecules beneath it with enough strength to hold up these very long columns of fluid within the xylem cells.

The shape of a leaf will help you identify the tree on which you find it. But one thing is certain—the shape of a leaf is not important when it comes to food production. Despite the many shapes and sizes of leaves, they all seem to work very well.

As you now know, leaves owe their green color to the pigment chlorophyll. However, many leaves also have pigments of other colors. A red pigment mixed with the green will give leaves a copper color. The copper beech is named for the distinctive color of its leaves. In the fall, when chlorophyll production drops, many trees reveal the other colored pigments that were previously hidden by the abundant chlorophyll. The result is the brilliant reds, oranges, and yellows that make up the autumn foliage in many parts of the United States.

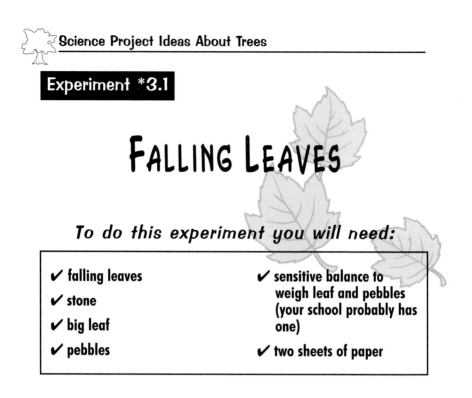

Experiment *3.1

FALLING LEAVES

To do this experiment you will need:

- ✔ falling leaves
- ✔ stone
- ✔ big leaf
- ✔ pebbles
- ✔ sensitive balance to weigh leaf and pebbles (your school probably has one)
- ✔ two sheets of paper

Autumn is a good time to watch leaves falling from trees. Do they seem to fall straight to the ground, or do they zigzag back and forth as they fall?

Drop a leaf and a stone at the same time. Which one falls faster? Did the stone fall faster because it is heavier? To find out, weigh a big leaf. Then weigh a number of small pebbles, one at a time, until you find one that weighs just about as much as the leaf. Drop the pebble and the leaf at the same time. Do they fall at the same time now, or does the pebble still fall faster? Is it weight that makes a stone fall faster than a leaf?

Take two sheets of paper and crumple one into a ball. Hold the crumpled sheet in one hand and the flat sheet in the other hand at the same height above the floor. Release both pieces of paper at the same time. Which one falls faster? Which one pushed against more air as it fell?

How can you measure the speed of a falling leaf?

DID YOU KNOW. . .?

In a vacuum, leaves fall as fast as lead spheres. It is the resistance offered by air that causes leaves to fall much more slowly than denser objects with less surface.

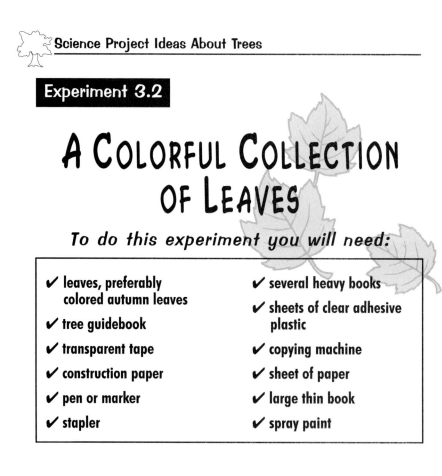

Experiment 3.2

A COLORFUL COLLECTION OF LEAVES

To do this experiment you will need:

- ✔ leaves, preferably colored autumn leaves
- ✔ tree guidebook
- ✔ transparent tape
- ✔ construction paper
- ✔ pen or marker
- ✔ stapler
- ✔ several heavy books
- ✔ sheets of clear adhesive plastic
- ✔ copying machine
- ✔ sheet of paper
- ✔ large thin book
- ✔ spray paint

Observing the shape and structure of a tree's leaves is a good way to identify a tree. And autumn is a good time to collect and preserve leaves from a variety of trees because the leaves at that time of year may be colorful. But it is important to do this activity safely. **AVOID POISONOUS LEAVES SUCH AS POISON IVY AND POISON SUMAC!** It would be a good idea to have someone show you what poison ivy looks like (see Figure 11a) before you begin collecting leaves. The same goes for poison sumac (see Figure 11b), though

FIGURE 11

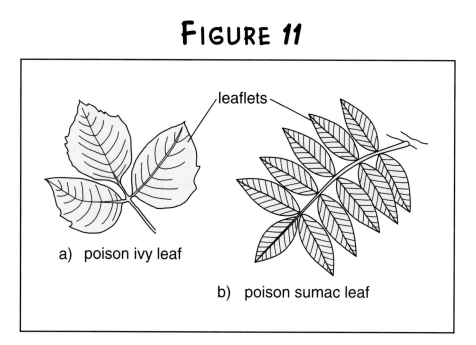

leaflets

a) poison ivy leaf

b) poison sumac leaf

Both poison ivy and poison sumac can cause serious skin irritation. Stay away from them!

a) Poison ivy is a shrub or climbing vine. Its leaves consist of three shiny leaflets. The leaflets are 2.5–10 cm (1–4 in) long and may have smooth or bluntly toothed edges. In late summer or fall it produces grayish berries.

b) Poison sumac is a shrub or short tree found in swamps or wet ground. Its leaves are 30–60 cm (1–2 ft) long with 7–13 leaflets, each 5–8 cm (2–3 in) long. The shiny leaflets have red veins and smooth edges.

it is less widely spread than poison ivy, which occurs throughout North America.

If possible, collect leaves in the fall so you can include leaves that are red, orange, yellow, and of mixed colors. You can select leaves from trees that you can identify by sight or with a tree guidebook. Try to collect some leaves that have only one blade such as oak, magnolia, and maple leaves. These are called simple leaves (see Figure 12). Try to find some compound leaves as well. Compound leaves have a number of blades (leaflets). The leaves of ash, walnut, locust, and horse chestnut trees are examples of compound leaves.

Use transparent tape to mount the leaves on sheets of construction paper. You can probably put several leaves on one sheet of paper. Label each leaf with the name of the tree from which it came.

After you have mounted all the leaves, staple the pages along one long edge, as shown in Figure 13. To prevent the leaves from curling as they dry, place the leaf book on a table and put several heavy books on top of it. After several weeks, the leaves should be dry and flat. You can then remove the books.

Another way to preserve leaves is to place them between two sheets of clear adhesive plastic. Hardware stores sell such a material

FIGURE 12

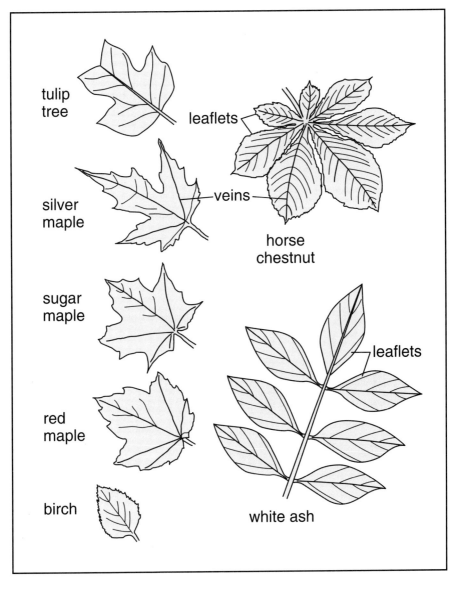

tulip tree

silver maple

sugar maple

red maple

birch

leaflets

veins

horse chestnut

leaflets

white ash

The leaves on the left are simple leaves. Those on the right are examples of compound leaves.

FIGURE 13

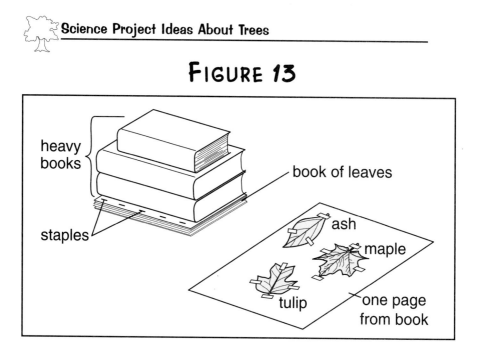

Use small pieces of transparent tape to mount leaves on sheets of paper. Staple the sheets together to make a leaf book. Then put a pile of heavy books on the leaf book to prevent the leaves from curling as they dry.

for lining kitchen shelves and drawers. If the leaves have their stunning autumn colors, you might like to mount them in a bright window.

Leaf silhouettes are easy to make. Simply place one or more leaves on a copying machine. Cover with a sheet of paper, place a large but thin book on the paper to keep the leaf flat, and make a copy. You can also make leaf silhouettes by placing leaves on a sheet of paper outdoors and spraying around them lightly with paint. Carefully remove the leaves and let the paint on the paper dry.

Experiment 3.3

LEAVES AND THEIR VEINS

To do this experiment you will need:

- ✔ several leaves from a single species of trees
- ✔ leaves from a number of different species of trees
- ✔ paper and pencil

Look closely at a leaf. You will see that it has lots of lines within it. These lines are called veins. The veins carry water and minerals to the leaf. They also carry food manufactured in the leaves to other parts of the tree. Veins serve as a skeleton for leaves. They keep it spread out and stiff so that it can receive more sunlight. How are the veins in trees similar to your veins? How are they different?

Collect leaves from several trees of a single species. Are the vein patterns in leaves the same for the same species? For example, do red maple leaves all have a similar vein pattern?

Collect leaves from a number of different species of trees. Do leaves from different species of trees have different vein patterns? Draw the leaf shapes and vein patterns for a number of different trees. Look at the vein patterns and leaf shapes shown in Figure 12. Did you collect leaves from any of the trees whose leaves are shown in those drawings? If you did, do your drawings resemble the ones shown in Figure 12?

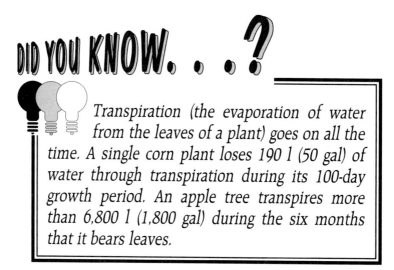

Transpiration (the evaporation of water from the leaves of a plant) goes on all the time. A single corn plant loses 190 l (50 gal) of water through transpiration during its 100-day growth period. An apple tree transpires more than 6,800 l (1,800 gal) during the six months that it bears leaves.

Experiment *3.4

LIGHT, LEAVES, AND CHLOROPHYLL

To do this experiment you will need:

- ✔ short board
- ✔ green grass
- ✔ aluminum foil or heavy black construction paper
- ✔ geranium plant
- ✔ paper clips
- ✔ scissors

Chlorophyll is the pigment that gives leaves their green color. It is also the chemical that plants need to produce food. Most of the food production (photosynthesis) goes on in the leaves when sunlight shines on them. Without light, food will not be produced. Photosynthesis will stop. But will chlorophyll still be present? Will the leaf keep its green color without light?

To find out, you can carry out two easy experiments. In the first experiment, simply place a short board on some green grass. Be sure you ask permission first.

In the second experiment, use heavy black construction paper or aluminum foil to cover one leaf of a geranium plant, as shown in

Figure 14. Choose a leaf that is exposed to sunlight most of the day. Fold the edges of the aluminum foil or paper and hold it in place with paper clips to be sure that no light reaches the leaf.

After a week of sunny weather, lift the board off the grass. Compare the grass that was under the board with grass that was not covered. How do they compare?

At this time, you can also remove the aluminum foil or paper that covered the geranium leaf. How does the leaf that was covered compare with a leaf that was exposed to light? What do these two experiments tell you? Is light needed for chlorophyll to be made in leaves?

FIGURE 14

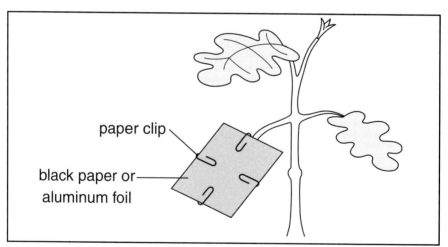

paper clip

black paper or aluminum foil

Does a leaf need light to produce chlorophyll?

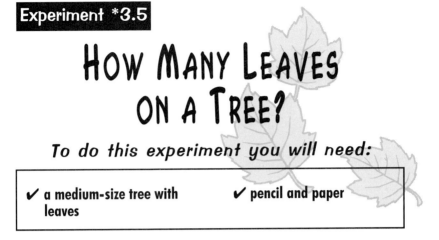

Experiment *3.5

HOW MANY LEAVES ON A TREE?

To do this experiment you will need:

- ✔ a medium-size tree with leaves
- ✔ pencil and paper

One answer to the question "How many leaves are on a tree?" might be "Lots of them!" But you can do better than that. You can make a reasonable estimate of the number of leaves on a tree.

To begin, count and record the number of leaves on several typical branches of a tree. To find the average number of leaves on a typical branch, add the number of leaves on all the branches you counted. Then divide this total by the number of branches. What is the average number of leaves on a branch?

Next, count the total number of branches on the tree. How can you use the average number of leaves per branch and the total number of branches to estimate the number of leaves on the tree? What is your estimate of the total number of leaves on the tree?

Make an estimate of the total number of leaves on all the trees on your street.

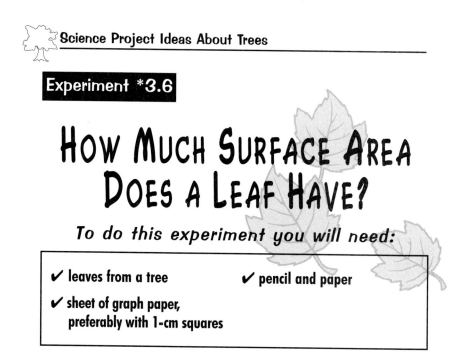

Experiment *3.6

HOW MUCH SURFACE AREA DOES A LEAF HAVE?

To do this experiment you will need:

- ✔ leaves from a tree
- ✔ sheet of graph paper, preferably with 1-cm squares
- ✔ pencil and paper

The total surface area of a tree's leaves is important. It is important because the leaves are where carbon dioxide and water react with chlorophyll in the presence of sunlight to form food and release oxygen. The greater the surface area, the greater the amount of food that can be manufactured in the leaves.

To find the surface area of a typical leaf, collect a number of leaves from one of the trees whose leaves you counted in the previous experiment. Place one of the leaves on a sheet of graph paper. Use a pencil to draw the outline of the leaf on the graph paper.

What is the area of one of the squares on the graph paper? For example, if the squares are 1.0 cm on a side, each square has an area of 1.0 square centimeter (1.0 cm x 1.0 cm = 1.0 sq cm). If the squares are 0.5 cm on a side, the area of each square is 0.25 sq cm (0.5 cm x 0.5 cm = 0.25 sq cm).

Count the number of squares covered by the typical leaf. (In some cases, you will have to estimate the fraction of one or more squares that are partially covered by the leaf. Add these fractions to the squares that are totally covered by the leaf.) What is the approximate area of the leaf in square centimeters?

How can you estimate the total surface area of all the leaves on a tree? What is the total area of the leaves on a tree?

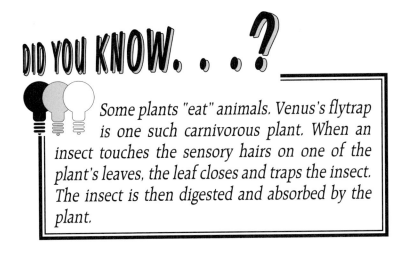

DID YOU KNOW. . .?

Some plants "eat" animals. Venus's flytrap is one such carnivorous plant. When an insect touches the sensory hairs on one of the plant's leaves, the leaf closes and traps the insect. The insect is then digested and absorbed by the plant.

Experiment *3.7

THE HOLES IN LEAVES

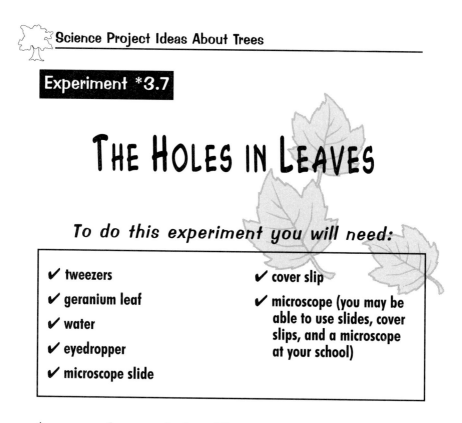

To do this experiment you will need:

- ✔ tweezers
- ✔ geranium leaf
- ✔ water
- ✔ eyedropper
- ✔ microscope slide
- ✔ cover slip
- ✔ microscope (you may be able to use slides, cover slips, and a microscope at your school)

As you learned in Chapter 1, leaves have openings called stomates. It is through these openings that gases such as carbon dioxide, oxygen, and water vapor pass into and out of the leaves.

To see the stomates, use tweezers to peel away a small piece of the thin "skin" on the underside of a geranium leaf. Place this thin skin of leaf tissue in a drop of water on a microscope slide. Then cover the drop and tissue with a glass or plastic cover slip. Look at the tissue under a microscope. You will see that the tiny stomates are surrounded by cells. These cells, shown in Figure 15, are called

FIGURE 15

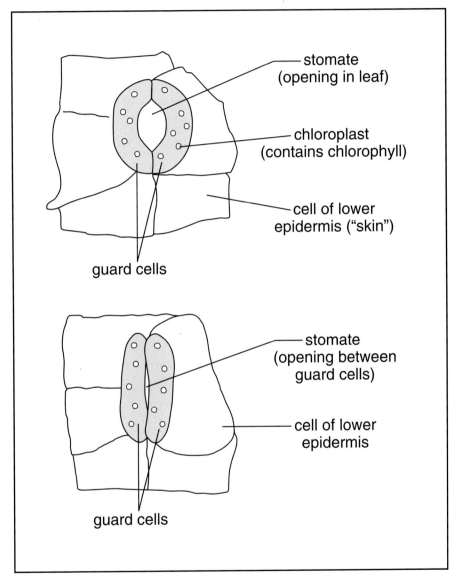

a) Guard cells swell when filled with water, creating an opening (stomate) between them.

b) Guard cells flatten after they have lost much of their water, closing the space between them.

guard cells. When the guard cells lose water, their shape changes and they close the stomates. When there is plenty of water, the guard cells are swollen, leaving an opening (stomate) between them.

Design an experiment to find the number of stomates on a leaf.

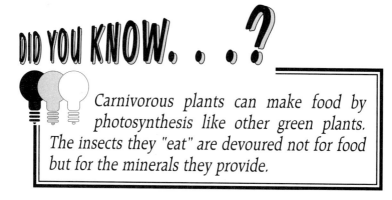

DID YOU KNOW. . .?

Carnivorous plants can make food by photosynthesis like other green plants. The insects they "eat" are devoured not for food but for the minerals they provide.

If a tree dies, plant another in its place.
(Carl von Linne [Linnaeus])

4

TREES, FRUITS, SEEDS, AND FLOWERS

Flowers are the reproductive organs of many trees. It is within a flower that the sperm from pollen unites with the egg cells within an ovule to form the seeds that grow into the next generation of these trees. To ensure the mixing of genes, which is essential for evolution, most trees have ways to prevent the pollen from a flower's stamens from falling on the pistils of the same flower. For example, the pollen and ovules may ripen at different times; the pollen may be unable to develop on pistils from the same tree; the tree may produce only staminate or pistillate flowers; or, in the case of pines, the pollen-bearing cones are on the lower branches so the pollen cannot fall on the female cones on the upper branches.

The pollen of most forest trees is carried to other flowers by the wind. Their flowers are generally rather drab and have little if any odor. It is trees such as the cherry, apple, magnolia, willow, and most ornamental trees that produce beautiful flowers with lovely odors. These trees must attract the insects that transport their pollen from flower to flower.

When a sperm from a pollen tube joins an egg in the pistil's ovule, the resulting embryo plant begins to develop and the ovule becomes a seed. Meanwhile the ovary, which surrounds the seed or seeds, begins to ripen. It is the ovary and sometimes other parts of the flower as well that become the fruit.

The seeds of gymnosperms are not covered by an ovary (see Figure 16). However, the seeds of some gymnosperms, such as the juniper, do have a fleshy cover. But the cover comes from the stalk, not the flower.

FIGURE 16

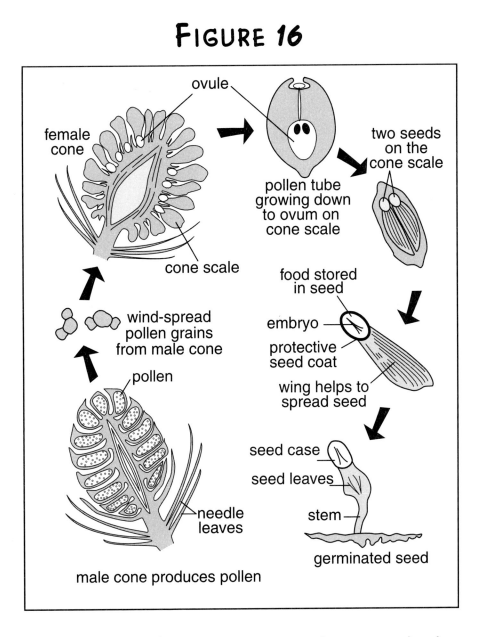

In the life cycle of gymnosperms, sperm and eggs are produced in separate cones, which may or may not be on the same tree.

Producing fruit is an advantage to the tree. The fruit will enable the seeds to be moved away from the tree. Berries, acorns, apples, and other fruits are eaten by animals. The seeds pass through the animals' digestive systems and are deposited far from the tree that produced them. Squirrels gather and hoard acorns in the fall. In the process, they lose some in the ground. In effect, they plant the seeds for the oak trees. The likelihood of an acorn being planted and germinating is very small. But seeds are produced in such great numbers that if only one in a million germinates and survives, the oak population will remain unchanged. The same figures are true for most other trees.

Some trees have still different ways of spreading their seeds. Alders grow near water. Their seeds contain tiny air-filled bladders. When the seeds fall, many are carried by the water to a damp shore where some of them may germinate. Maples and ash trees produce winged seeds that spin and wobble as they fall, enabling the wind to carry them from beneath the limbs of their parents. The fruit of the witch hazel has a built-in spring mechanism. When the fruit dries and opens, it projects the seeds away from the plant. Willows and poplars have developed what may be the best means of spreading seeds. Their seeds, like those of the dandelion, are light with a fluffy material that acts like a parachute. If caught by the wind, they may be carried for miles.

Seeds, which are usually produced in the late summer or fall, remain dormant during the winter. In fact, seeds may remain dormant for a long time—some for as long as a thousand years.

A seed contains a tiny new plant—the embryo. It also encloses enough food to enable the young plant to grow a root into the soil and absorb water and minerals. The water causes

FIGURE 17

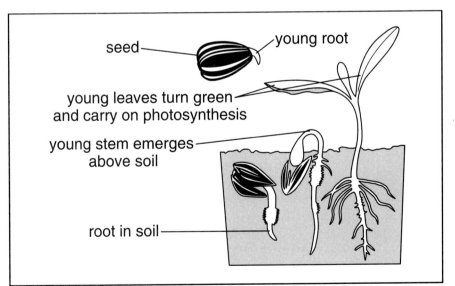

A seed germinates to become a seedling.

the seed tissue to swell, pushing the root and stem through the soil. The young leaves then open, as shown in Figure 17. Once the seedling has leaves and light, it can carry on photosynthesis and produce its own food. With years of continued growth, it will become a tree and produce its own flowers, fruits, and seeds.

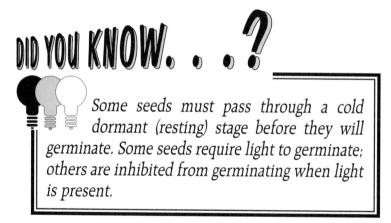

DID YOU KNOW. . .?

Some seeds must pass through a cold dormant (resting) stage before they will germinate. Some seeds require light to germinate; others are inhibited from germinating when light is present.

Experiment 4.1

FLOWERS

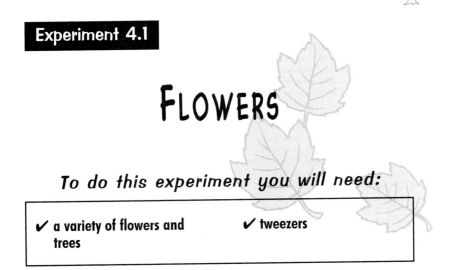

To do this experiment you will need:

- ✔ a variety of flowers and trees
- ✔ tweezers

Examine the flowers on several different kinds of plants. A typical flower was shown in Figure 1. You can probably identify the petals (if they are present) and the sepals, which are under the petals. It's easy to identify the flower parts of a tulip or the flowers on a fruit tree, so you might start with them, if possible.

With permission, pick several flowers. How many sepals does the flower have? Do all flowers have the same number of sepals? Use tweezers to remove the sepals and petals. How many petals did the flower have? Do all flowers have the same number of petals? Next, remove the stamens. How many were there? Does the flower have one pistil, or more than one? Break open the pistil. Can you find an ovule inside?

Can you find flowers on trees in the spring? (Figure 18 shows the flowers produced by

FIGURE 18

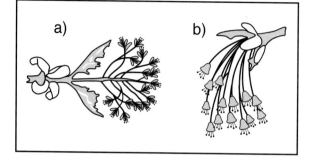

The flowers of a) Norway maple and b) sugar maple trees are shown.

sugar maples and Norway maples.) Can you find pistils and stamens in the flowers? Remember, many trees have separate male and female flowers. In some cases, a tree will have only staminate flowers or only pistillate flowers. Can you find trees, such as pussy willows, that have only male or female flowers?

Can you find the cones on evergreen trees such as pines?

Can you figure out how the pollen is transferred from stamens to pistils? Is it carried by the wind? by insects? by birds or other animals? by water? by gravity? by some other means?

Continue to watch the trees whose flowers you have identified. You will see some of the flowers, or the female flowers, turn into fruits that enclose the seeds. Watch for the seeds to fall from the tree. How are the seeds dispersed? Can you find any seeds that have germinated?

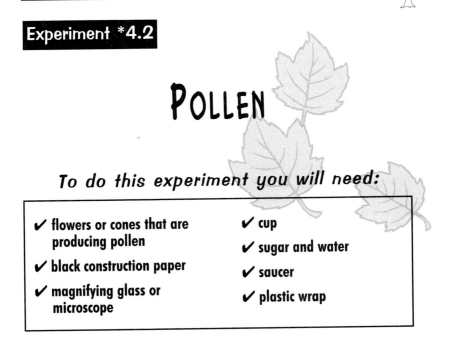

Experiment *4.2

POLLEN

To do this experiment you will need:

- ✔ flowers or cones that are producing pollen
- ✔ black construction paper
- ✔ magnifying glass or microscope
- ✔ cup
- ✔ sugar and water
- ✔ saucer
- ✔ plastic wrap

Find flowers that have pollen on their stamens, or pine cones that shed a fine yellow powder (pollen) when shaken. Gently shake the pollen onto a small piece of black construction paper. Use a strong magnifying glass or a microscope to look at the pollen grains. Compare the pollen grains from different flowers and cones. How do they differ? Do any resemble those shown in Figure 19a?

Dissolve several tablespoonsful of sugar in a cup of water. Pour a little of the sugar solution into a shallow saucer. Sprinkle some of the pollen onto the sugar water. Cover the saucer with plastic wrap and leave it in a warm place for several hours.

FIGURE 19

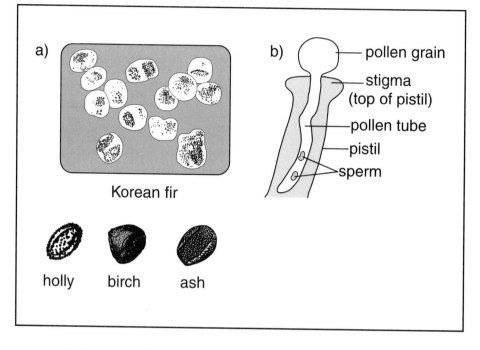

a) Pollen grains from several different trees are shown. The pollen has been greatly magnified. The Korean fir pollen grains have balloonlike air sacs that enable them to almost float in air.

b) A pollen tube grows from a pollen grain and carries sperm to the egg inside a flower's pistil.

Examine the pollen grains with a magnifying glass or microscope. Can you see any tubes like the ones shown in Figure 19b growing from the pollen grains? These are the tubes that grow into the pistil and reach the ovules in the ovary.

Experiment *4.3

FRUITS AND SEEDS

To do this experiment you will need:

- ✔ variety of fruits
- ✔ an ADULT
- ✔ knife
- ✔ variety of angiosperm trees
- ✔ soil
- ✔ wooden coffee stirrers
- ✔ pen or marker
- ✔ gymnosperm trees
- ✔ tree guidebook
- ✔ green pine cones

The seeds of angiosperm trees are found inside the fruit. With time and patience, you can collect a large number of seeds produced by different trees. You know where to look for the seeds of apple, orange, lemon, lime, grapefruit, peach, pear, and cherry trees.

If possible, collect some of the fruits shown in Figure 20. As you can see from the drawings, there are many types of fruit. The words commonly used to describe a fruit do not always agree with the scientific definitions. For example, neither a raspberry nor a strawberry is a true berry. One is an aggregate

FIGURE 20

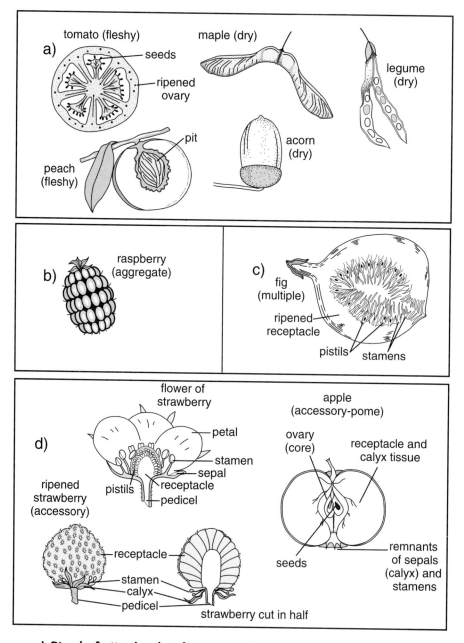

a) Simple fruits develop from a single ovary. b) Aggregate fruits are those where several ovaries on the same flower ripen together. c) In multiple fruits many ovaries from separate flowers ripen together on one stem. d) Accessory fruits include parts of the flower or plant other than the ovary.

fruit, the other an accessory fruit. But a tomato is a berry. Can you explain why?

Examine as many different types of fruit as you can. **ASK AN ADULT** to cut open fleshy fruits so you can look inside. The dry fruits can be examined as they are. Can you find the seeds? Can you find any flower parts, other than the ovary, that still remain with the fruit?

Many trees, such as the horse chestnut, oak, beech, black walnut, butternut, pecan, and hickory, produce a fruit called a nut that contains the tree's seed. Can you find any trees that produce nuts?

If there are maple trees near where you live, look for hanging clusters of their winged seeds late in the spring or in the summer. They eventually fall from the tree. It's fun to watch them spin as they fall. Sometimes the wind carries them far away. How are the seeds from other trees dispersed (scattered) so that they don't grow in the shade of their parent tree?

Locust, catalpa, Kentucky coffee, mesquite, and palo verde trees produce a podlike fruit, similar to pea pods, that have several seeds inside. Look for these pods in late summer. When the pods dry, you can open them and see the seeds inside.

Plant some different kinds of tree seeds in soil. Use a wooden coffee stirrer to label each seed you plant. Do any of the seeds germinate and grow?

The seeds of gymnosperms (evergreens, conifers, softwoods—trees with needlelike leaves) are found inside their cones. Once the cones open, the seeds can be found on the scales of the cone or on the ground beneath the tree.

How many different kinds of cones can you find? Use a tree guidebook to help you identify the species that produced them. Are the trees that produced each kind of cone nearby?

Find some pine cones that are still green. Take them into your home or school and let them dry. When the cones are dry and open, you can see the seeds on the scales of the cones.

GERMINATING SEEDS AND ROOT HAIRS

To do this experiment you will need:

- ✔ water
- ✔ paper towels
- ✔ wide soup dish
- ✔ radish or mustard seeds
- ✔ plastic wrap
- ✔ magnifying glass

The roots of a tree provide support and anchor the plant to the ground. Roots also absorb water and minerals from the soil in which a tree grows. In this experiment, you will see the tiny roots where fluids enter a plant.

Place a moist paper towel on the bottom of a wide soup dish. Sprinkle a few radish or mustard seeds on the paper. Then cover the dish with plastic wrap, as shown in Figure 21a. The plastic wrap should keep the paper from drying out, but check daily to be sure the towel is moist. If the towel appears to be drying, add enough water to keep it moist. After several days, the seeds should begin to germinate. You will see tiny roots emerging from the seeds.

FIGURE 21

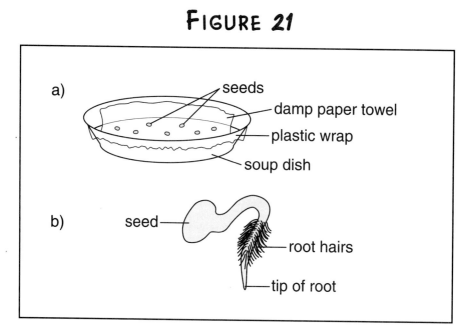

a) Seeds will germinate on a damp paper towel.

b) Root hairs grow near the root tip of a germinating seed.

FIGURE 22

The roots seen on this tree were once underground. But the topsoil eroded, leaving some of the roots exposed.

As the roots grow, look for fuzzy regions to develop just behind the tips of the roots. Remove the plastic wrap and use a magnifying glass to look closely at the fuzzy region (Figure 21b). It is made up of tiny root hairs. It is through these root hairs that water and minerals enter a plant. Even trees with huge roots, like the ones you can see in Figure 22, absorb fluids through root hairs at the ends of their smallest roots.

Under the spreading chestnut tree
The village smithy stands . . .
(Henry Wadsworth Longfellow)

5

How Trees Grow

A tree is different from other plants. It forms an upright "skeleton" of wood from which grow its leaves, flowers, and fruit. Each year it adds more height and breadth to its own woody skeleton. By summer, the buds that will produce growth during the following spring have already been formed. They remain dormant throughout the fall and winter. In the spring they will emerge as the days lengthen and as the sun, now higher in the sky, provides added warmth.

FIGURE 23

a) When this pine tree was young, a large tree fell on it. The young tree was bent in such a way that it formed a loop as it continued to grow, always "reaching" for light.

b) The limb of the tree on the left grew until it touched the tree on the right. As the limb and trunk rubbed against each other, the bark on both wore off. Sap from the two trees helped fuse them together.

But not all the buds will develop. The ones farthest from the roots grow upward and outward the fastest. The other buds become the support for leaves and flowers or are held in reserve should the farthest buds be damaged or lost.

As the photographs in Figure 23 reveal, trees can sometimes grow in funny ways.

Experiment *5.1

WHAT PARTS OF A TREE GROW?

To do this experiment you will need:

- ✔ colored yarn
- ✔ small tree
- ✔ thumbtack
- ✔ tape measure
- ✔ notebook
- ✔ pen or pencil

Tree rings show us that a tree's trunk grows thicker each year. But does a tree grow in other places?

To find out, begin this experiment in late winter before the trees begin to form new leaves. Tie a piece of colored yarn a few centimeters from the tip of a twig on a small tree. At the same time, push a thumbtack into the tree's main trunk. Use a tape measure to find the distance between the thumbtack and the ground. Use the same tape to measure the distance between the yarn and the tip of the twig. Finally, measure the small tree's height. Record these three measurements in a notebook.

The next fall, after the trees have shed most of their leaves, again measure the distance between the yarn and the tip of the twig. Has the distance changed? Also measure the height of the thumbtack from the ground and the height of the small tree. Which, if any, of these measurements indicate growth?

Based on your measurements, where does growth occur in a tree other than across its trunk? If you hung a swing from the limb of a large tree, would the swing's seat be too high after a few years?

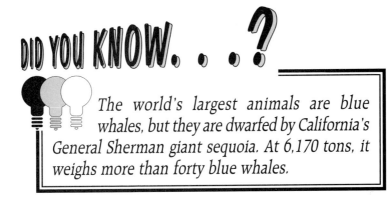

DID YOU KNOW. . .?

The world's largest animals are blue whales, but they are dwarfed by California's General Sherman giant sequoia. At 6,170 tons, it weighs more than forty blue whales.

Experiment *5.2

BUDS AND TWIGS

To do this experiment you will need:

- ✔ twigs cut from different kinds of trees
- ✔ garden pruner
- ✔ marking pen
- ✔ masking tape
- ✔ magnifying glass
- ✔ tweezers
- ✔ wide board
- ✔ glass tumblers or jars
- ✔ water
- ✔ warm sunny place
- ✔ warm dark place
- ✔ cool sunny place

Most angiosperm trees lose their leaves in the fall. But if you look closely at a tree in the winter, you can find the leaves that will appear next spring. The tiny leaves are enclosed in the buds. Ask permission to pick or cut a few twigs from some different trees. A garden pruner can be used to cut the twigs. Try to find twigs that have large buds like the ones shown in Figure 24. When you cut a twig, try to identify the tree from which it came so that you can label it. Write the name of the tree on a piece of masking tape. Attach the tape to the twig so that you will be able to identify it later.

FIGURE 24

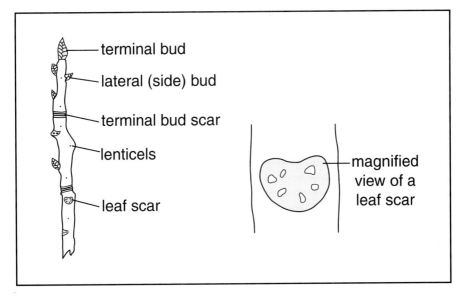

A twig from a horse chestnut tree shows a terminal bud, lateral buds, terminal bud scars, leaf scars, and lenticels.

Take the twigs inside where it is warm. Use a magnifying glass to look closely at a large bud. You will see that it has large brown scales that protect the tissues under it. Use your fingers or a pair of tweezers to remove the brown scales. Under the scales you should find a number of tiny leaves. How many leaves can you find inside a bud? Does the number depend on the kind of tree?

The buds at the end of a twig are called terminal buds. The buds along the sides of a twig are called lateral buds. Are lateral and terminal buds the same or different inside?

As you were looking at the buds, you may have noticed scars along the twig. The small scars with little dots in the middle are called leaf scars. The ones shown in Figure 24 are on a horse chestnut twig, where the scars are heart-shaped and very easy to see. Leaf scars are left by leaves that have fallen from the tree. Typical leaf scars from a number of different trees are shown in Figure 25. The dots are the remains of tubes that ran through the leaf's stem. The tubes carried water, minerals, and food between the leaves and the stem (twig).

Other dots that you see on the twig are called lenticels. They are openings that let air into the stem tissue.

Can you find the scars left by terminal buds on your twigs? The length of the twig from one terminal bud scar to the next marks the twig's growth during a one-year period. How much did one of your twigs grow last year?

If you have a good variety of twigs, mount them on a board and label them. You might like to exhibit your twig collection in a small nature museum you can make at school or at home.

FIGURE 25

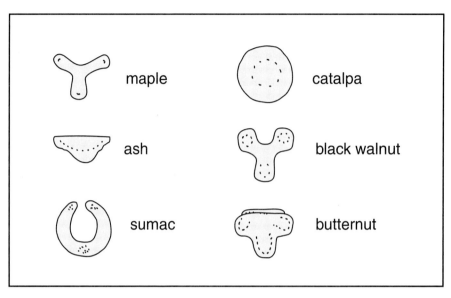

Here are some different shapes of leaf scars from different kinds of trees.

You may be able to make some of the buds on the twigs open. Winter buds on twigs from maple and willow trees will almost always bloom if you place the twigs in a glass of water in a warm sunny place. To help water enter the twigs, use a garden pruner to cut about 3 cm (1 in) from the lower end of the twigs when you put them in the water. The cutting should be done underwater. Cut 1 cm (0.5 in) from the bottom of the twig each week. Do any of the buds produce flowers? Do any of the buds produce leaves?

Experiment *5.3

MEASURING TWIG GROWTH

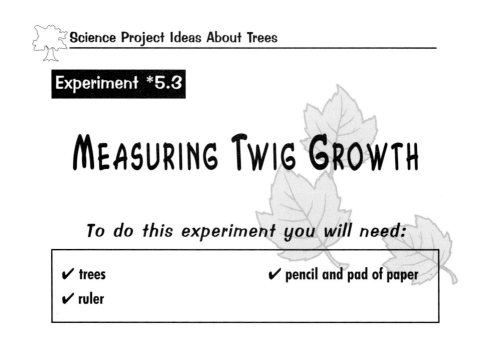

To do this experiment you will need:

✔ trees
✔ ruler

✔ pencil and pad of paper

In the previous experiment you found that terminal buds leave scars called terminal bud scars. The distance between the present terminal bud and the terminal bud scar nearest to it on the twig shows the twig's growth during the past year. The distance between two terminal bud scars on the same twig indicates a year's growth.

Go back to one of the trees from which you took twigs. Examine branches that you can reach from the ground. Look at branches on the tree's north, east, south, and west sides. If you don't know the directions at the tree where you are, just remember that south is the direction where the sun will be at noon. You can make a reasonable estimate of directions if you keep that in mind. **DO NOT LOOK DIRECTLY AT THE SUN! IT CAN DAMAGE YOUR EYES.**

Start at the present terminal bud on a twig on one side of the tree. Work back along the twig to the branch's terminal bud scars from one, two, three, four, or more years ago. Use a ruler to measure the amount of growth during each of the years that you can measure. Make measurements on branches from all four sides of the tree. Use pencil and paper to record your measurements. Your record might look like the one below.

KIND OF TREE	SIDE OF TREE	YEARS AGO	GROWTH
horse chestnut	south	1	14 cm
horse chestnut	south	2	12 cm

If possible, make or share measurements from several kinds of trees. Take your data back to your home or school and examine it carefully. Do branches grow the same amount each year? If not, which year in the recent past seemed to be the best for growth? Does direction (north, east, south, west) make a difference in the amount that branches grow in any one year? If it does, which direction seems to produce the most growth? the least growth? Are the results similar for all species of trees? If not, how do they differ?

Experiment *5.4

ANOTHER EXPERIMENT WITH TWIGS AND BUDS

To do this experiment you will need:

- ✔ 3 twigs from the same tree
- ✔ glass tumbler or jar
- ✔ water
- ✔ warm sunny place
- ✔ garden pruner
- ✔ an ADULT
- ✔ knife

Cut three twigs of similar size from the same tree. Place them in a glass of water in front of a warm sunny window. Remove the top (terminal) bud from one of the twigs. **ASK AN ADULT** to cut a slit halfway around a second twig just above one of the side (lateral) buds. Do nothing to the third twig; it will serve as a "control," one that you can compare with the others.

To help water enter the twigs, use a garden pruner to cut about 3 cm (1 in) from the lower end of the twigs when you put them in the water. The cutting should be done underwater.

Watch the three twigs over the next several weeks. Cut another centimeter (0.5 in) from the bottom of the twigs each week.

Compare the first and third twigs. What effect does the removal of the terminal bud have on the first twig's growth? What effect does it have on the other buds on the twig?

The cut around the second twig should reduce the flow of water and minerals going up the twig above the lateral bud. Does the lateral bud below the cut grow faster or slower than the other buds on the twig?

DID YOU KNOW. . .?

A tree is a tall woody plant that has one stem known as the trunk. A shrub is a woody plant with branches near the ground. It has no single trunk. An herb is a nonwoody plant that dies (at least above ground) in the winter.

Experiment *5.5

TREES AND THEIR LOCATION

To do this experiment you will need:

- ✔ trees of the same species located in different places
- ✔ pen or pencil
- ✔ notebook

Watch a number of trees of the same species over a period of one year or longer. Choose trees that are both large and small. Choose trees that are located in different places such as a hill, a valley, a shady place, a sunny place, a wet place, a dry place, on the edge of a forest, inside a forest, on a lawn, etc. Make a map showing the location of your trees, and number each tree on the map. Notice and record such things as the time that leaves and flowers first appear on each tree; the time that leaves first begin to turn color in the autumn; the amount that the tree's branches grew in the past year; the side of the tree that is growing fastest and the side that is growing slowest; the trees that have the largest leaves; and other differences that you notice as you watch your trees.

Can you explain why one tree develops leaves first? Does it receive more light than the other trees? Does it receive more moisture? Is it more protected from the wind than the other trees?

Try to find possible explanations for the observations you make. Then design experiments to test your explanations. Do any of your experiments confirm your explanations? Do any of your experiments indicate that your first explanation was wrong? Do these experiments lead to other explanations?

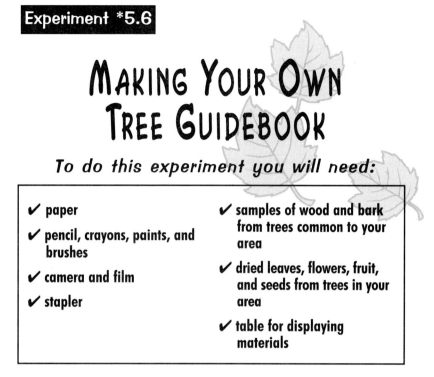

Experiment *5.6

MAKING YOUR OWN TREE GUIDEBOOK

To do this experiment you will need:

- ✔ paper
- ✔ pencil, crayons, paints, and brushes
- ✔ camera and film
- ✔ stapler
- ✔ samples of wood and bark from trees common to your area
- ✔ dried leaves, flowers, fruit, and seeds from trees in your area
- ✔ table for displaying materials

If you have a camera or some artistic talent, you might enjoy preparing a guidebook that will help people identify the different kinds of trees that are common in your town. Your paintings, drawings, photographs, or some combination of all of these could show the general shape of each tree, the shapes of their leaves, their bark, and their flowers, seeds, and fruit. Be sure to include labels and some descriptions to accompany your artwork and/or photographs. Actual samples of leaves, wood, bark, twigs, flowers, fruit, and seeds from the trees could be used to set up a small museum in your school or home.

FURTHER READING

Bonnet, Robert L., and G. Daniel Keen. *Botany: 49 Science Fair Projects.* Blue Ridge Summit, Penn.: TAB Books, 1989.

Gardner, Robert. *Make an Interactive Science Museum: Hands-On Exhibits!* New York: TAB Books, 1996.

Johnson, Hugh. *Hugh Johnson's Encyclopedia of Trees.* New York: Gallery Books, 1984.

Lawrence, Eleanor, and Cecilia Fitzsimons. *An Instant Guide to Trees.* Stamford, Conn.: Longmeadow Press, 1991.

Prochnow, Dave, and Kathy Prochnow. *Why?: Experiments for the Young Scientist.* Blue Ridge Summit, Penn.: TAB Books, 1993.

Rushforth, Keith. *Nature Library: Trees.* New York: Exeter Books, 1983.

Simon and Schuster's Guide to Trees. New York: Simon and Schuster, 1977.

Taylor's Guide to Trees. New York: Chanticleer Press, 1988.

Webster, David. *Exploring Nature Around the Year: Fall.* New York: Julian Messner, 1989.

Webster, David. *Exploring Nature Around the Year: Spring.* New York: Julian Messner, 1989.

Webster, David. *Exploring Nature Around the Year: Winter.* New York: Julian Messner, 1989.

LIST OF MATERIALS

A
aluminum foil

B
balance
bark
board
books
branches
bucket

C
calculator
camera
celery stalk
coffee stirrers
concrete block
construction paper
copying machine
cover slip
crayon
cutting board

E
eyedropper

F
film
firewood
flowers
food coloring
friend
fruits

G
garden pruner
geranium plant
glasses
graph paper
grass
green pine cones

H
hammer

J
jars

K
knife

L
leaves

M
magnifying glass
marker
measuring cup
meterstick
microscope
microscope slide

N
nails
newspaper
notebook

O
oak board

P
paintbrushes
paints
paper
paper clips
paper towels
pebbles
pencil
pine board
plastic sheets
plastic wrap
pliers

R
rope
ruler

S
saucer
saw
scale
scissors
seeds
shovel
sink
soil
soup dish
spray paint
stapler
stone
sugar
sun

T
tape
tape measure
thumbtack
tree guidebook
tree stump
trees
tweezers
twig

W
water
wood
workbench

Y
yarn

INDEX

A
angiosperms, 6, 71
annual rings, 16, 30–33
apple, 6

B
buds, 78–90

C
chlorophyll, 12, 43, 53–54
Christmas trees, 34–35
cones, 6, 15, 74
cord of wood, 39

D
density of wood, 37–41

E
egg, 8

F
flowers, 6–9, 15, 61–62, 67–68
forest areas, 18
fruit, 6, 71–73
    types of, 72–73

G
guidebook for trees, 93
gymnosperms, 6, 62, 74

H
heartwood, 22–23

L
leaves, 12–14, 42–60
    collecting, 46–50
    compound, 48–49
    falling, 44–45
    preserving, 49–50
    simple, 48–49
    surface area, 56–57
    time on tree, 55
    veins, 51–52

O
ovary, 6

P
photosynthesis, 12, 53
pistil, 6
poison ivy, 46–47
poison sumac, 46–47
pollen, 8, 61–63, 69–70

R
root hairs, 76–77
roots, 14–15

S
sapwood, 22–23
seeds, 6, 16, 61–66
    abundance of, 64

distribution of, 64–65
germination, 75–77
winged, 64
stem, 10–12
stomates, 14, 58–60
stump rubbings, 32

T
trees
    age of, 30–33
    Christmas, 34–35
    deciduous, 8
    definition of, 6
    growth of, 16, 80–90
    guidebook, 93
    height, 21, 24–29
    location, 91–92
    measuring, 24–29
    parts, 9
    products, 5
    trunk cross section, 22
twigs, 80–90

W
wood
    cord of, 39
    density, 37–41
    hardness, 36
    heat content, 40–41